FOUR PLAYS
FOR
COARSE ACTORS

by

MICHAEL GREEN

Performed at the Edinburgh Festival 1977 as
The Coarse Acting Show

SAMUEL  FRENCH

LONDON

NEW YORK   TORONTO   SYDNEY   HOLLYWOOD

MADE AND PRINTED IN GREAT BRITAIN BY
LATIMER TREND & COMPANY LTD PLYMOUTH
MADE IN ENGLAND

FOUR PLAYS FOR COARSE ACTORS
(THE COARSE ACTING SHOW)

INTRODUCTION   v

IL FORNICAZIONE   1

STREUTH   13

A COLLIER'S TUESDAY TEA   27

ALL'S WELL THAT ENDS AS YOU LIKE IT   41

FURNITURE AND PROPERTY LISTS   57

There is no need to play these pieces in the order given here. The running order for *The Coarse Acting Show* at Edinburgh was *Streuth, Il Fornicazione, A Collier's Tuesday Tea, All's Well That Ends As You Like It.*

AUTHOR'S NOTE

It is recommended that *Streuth* should open any Coarse Acting Show, as it is the archetypal amateur detective drama and firmly sets the scene for the audience. Some societies have been successful in giving the show a particular theme, such as the idea that it is an evening to raise funds to repair the church hall sanitation, complete with introduction by the "vicar". A Glasgow group played the show as if produced as therapy by reformed psychopathic convicts. But the show doesn't necessarily need gimmicks, although they can be very funny if they work. At Edinburgh we simply tried to make people feel they were at a serious, sincere evening of plays at a local hall by a not very talented group. Our sound operator set the mood with a version of the National Anthem as taken from a very old disc, which started, stopped and finally wheezed to a halt. The introductory music to *Streuth* was somewhat similar.

The stage directions in the plays indicate how they were originally played. But there are many different interpretations possible, and having seen several performances since this volume was first published I have been very impressed by the way in which directors and actors have brought out different aspects, such as the actor in *Streuth* who stood up every time he spoke. There is plenty of scope for innovation. In *A Collier's Tuesday Tea*, for instance, one group played Grandpa as Grandma. Another company used a cardboard stag in *Il Fornicazione*, with hilarious effect.

Since first publication of this show I have taken a sequel to Edinburgh, The Coarse Acting Show 2, which also consists of four short plays, and this was later transferred to the Shaftesbury Theatre, London. Companies might find a mixture of plays from the two shows would make a suitable evening.

M. G.

INTRODUCTION

What are Coarse Actors? And why write plays for them? It all began with my book *The Art of Coarse Acting*, a sort of text-book of stage disaster and moronic performance. It seemed to strike a chord with many stage people, both amateur and professional. Some wrote with experiences of their own, such as a Birmingham man who described a *Macbeth* in which the blades of Macbeth's property daggers fell off. Lady Macbeth, thinking she was being very resourceful, then pronounced:

> Infirm of purpose!
> Give me the handles!

and snatched them from a startled Macbeth.

Another actor claimed a colleague, in the typical way of a Coarse Actor, always made himself up in grotesque fashion and had all his disguises prepared in boxes from which he could produce any physical infirmity. Before a show he'd say, "Pass me my wart box, old chap" and plaster his face with warts, and then go to a tin labelled BOILS and add some of those, finishing off from a box with SCABS written on the lid. The final touch was a quick dusting with dandruff from a pepperpot. The writer said it was driving him mad using the same dressing-room.

Some performers found an irresistible desire to let their hair down and have a coarse acting orgy, which manifested itself in outbreaks of dramatic mayhem organized as Coarse Acting festivals. The first was at the Questors' Theatre, Ealing (at the suggestion of its founder, Alfred Emmet) and proved so popular that several more have been held. Others have been organized by various amateur groups and at professional theatres such as Salisbury Playhouse. These festivals gave rise to the idea of—and the demand for—plays especially written for Coarse Acting.

In *The Art of Coarse Acting* I give two definitions of a Coarse Actor: one who can remember the pauses but not the lines; or one who can remember the lines but not the order in which they come. But these describe only one facet of the Coarse Actor—his carelessness and incompetence. There is more to being a Coarse Actor than just being a bad actor. One of the things which distinguishes him is his desire to shine. Hence the man with a box full of warts. It is impossible for the audience to ignore even the smallest bit-part, if the man playing it has covered himself in warts and boils. I was reminded of this recently on watching an amateur group perform *The Beggar's Opera*. The show was ruined by a character with a parrot sewn on one shoulder who kept mowing and gibbering all over the stage at every conceivable opportunity. The director told me he knew he was going to have trouble when the man arrived at rehearsal and said, "Do you want me to wear my parrot sewn on the left or the right shoulder?"

As this actor showed another strong characteristic of the Coarse Actor—to be totally undirectable—the director had to put up with it. In fact he was lucky—my friend Askew usually straps up one leg and walks with a crutch no matter what part he is playing.

Laziness in learning lines (or inability to do so) is another characteristic of a Coarse Actor. This often leads to great ingenuity in concealing cribs. In *The Art of Coarse Acting* I have described a man who wrote his lines on playing-cards, which were used in a game on-stage. Alas, the vital card was trumped and shuffled into the pack with the result he was hurling cards in all directions when the cue came. Most of us have had the experience of pasting lines inside a newspaper only to find the props girl has changed the paper one night and you're faced with a choice of taking a prompt or reading out the football scores.

But no matter what disasters occur, the Coarse Actor believes it is all for the best. He really does think he—or she—is helping the show along. The Lady Macbeth who said, "Give me the handles" genuinely believed she had saved the situation instead of wrecking one of Shakespeare's greatest scenes. The stage manager whom I described in *Coarse Acting* as falling on stage glued to the back of a flat (The Human Cleat) blamed the flat, not himself. There is a good example of this in *Streuth*, where the Inspector, who believes himself to be the mainspring of the society, is responsible eventually for the play's downfall when in his nervousness he keeps repeating a cue with the result that the play goes round in circles. Painstaking earnestness is the trademark of some Coarse Actors.

The fact is, there is a little Coarse Acting in even the best performers and the best productions, waiting for its chance to jump out. The French have a word for it. They call it *Cabotinage*.

The Coarse Acting Festivals revealed some astonishing talent in this Black Art. Some entrants have written their own plays; others preferred to perform coarse productions of standard works. In this connection Shakespeare has naturally suffered a great deal, and one of the most memorable performances was a truncated version of *Hamlet* by the Maskers of Southampton, which won the 1974 Salisbury Playhouse Festival. This was notable for the fact that the ghost permanently dragged round a fifteen-foot length of chain behind him, and for a dense fog on the battlements which obliterated actors and audience, so all that could be discerned was an occasional spear passing through the murk, while Bernardo and Francesco bellowed at each other. There was also a splendid Polonius who spent his time in true Coarse fashion bent double, cackling and gibbering.

I mention this Polonius because he showed another Coarse characteristic—the tendency to make all characters stock parts. Thus all policemen tread like elephants, all old men quaver and gibber. Delicate shades and subtleties are unknown. Polonius is played exactly as Old Gobbo.

Another excellent piece was a version of the murder of Caesar from *Julius Caesar* by the Royal Shakespeare Company, who entered a talented two-man side of Tony Pedley and Roger Rees, at a Questors' competition. In this, Caesar (with several knives sticking from him and blood spouting all over the place) was pursued round the audience by Brutus, eventually escaping through the emergency exit with a cry of "Et tu, Brute" and a final squirt of blood. And I must also mention a murder mystery by The National Theatre team at Salisbury, where the butler visibly aged each time he entered the room, starting off about thirty-five and ending the play around eighty-eight.

But the most successful performances are those not far from reality. It cannot be stressed too strongly that Coarse Acting is at its funniest when it is nearest to the truth and when the actors are playing in deadly earnest. For Coarse Acting—the deliberately staged version that is—is not just sending up. Everyone is playing two parts—the part in the play and the person playing it. A Coarse Actor's Hamlet is not merely sending up Hamlet, he is acting the part of a chief clerk playing Hamlet and that is a different matter.

When these four plays were presented at the Edinburgh Festival Fringe as *The Coarse Acting Show* we invented a mythical society—The Ministry of Defence Players—and worked out each person's place in it. The Inspector in *Streuth* was a senior official and treasurer; the unfortunate clown in *All's Well That Ends As You Like It* was a down-trodden clerk (see Production Notes). If that sounds like taking it too seriously I can only say that after living with the plays for so long we began to see all sorts of new things and even discussed the sub-text, as if Coarse Acting was a branch of Drama (perhaps it is, and we should claim to be part of the Theatre of the Absurd).

At any rate, the lesson learned from competitions and Edinburgh is that the more seriously a Coarse Acting piece is taken by the cast, the better the result. The technique appeared to work at Edinburgh where we had full houses and excellent notices.

For the dividing line between Coarse Theatre and respectable theatre is thin and easily broken. Even professional directors are capable of over-doing the effects in *Hamlet* and I recall at least one West End production in which Hamlet moved with his own private cloud of dry ice following him around; the outrageous burlesque of Caesar's death was not so very far from some of Stratford's worst efforts and certainly little more exaggerated than a death scene I saw at the Old Vic in *King John* many years ago, which was so unintentionally hilarious that the audience cried "encore!".

Sometimes groups have preferred to write their own material. Pitton Theatre Club, Salisbury, wrote a delightful pastiche of an amateur musical and Bournemouth Little Theatre Club's whodunit was another memorable original piece (the murderer forgot the gun and offered his victim poison instead). Others have performed successfully in mime, like the company who did *War and Peace* in three minutes, omitting none of the plot.

As regards the plays in this volume, *Streuth*, performed (if that is the right word) by the Bunny Langridge Players from Ealing, won first prize in a Questors' tournament; *A Collier's Tuesday Tea*, by the same group, was highly commended at a subsequent festival. Later, *Streuth* became successful. While those in the studio fell about, the reaction of less sophisticated viewers is summed up by a neighbour who said, "Things kept going wrong in that there play by your friends . . ."

Both pieces were written by members of Questors who formed the Bunny Langridge Players for competition purposes. *Streuth* is a parody of the traditional french-window-and-vicar country crime mystery (I think). On the other hand it may be a criticism of the values of modern society. *A Collier's Tuesday Tea* bears some slight resemblance to a mining epic by D. H. Lawrence as performed by the local technical college.

The other two plays were written by myself. *Il Fornicazione*, a one-act opera, was inspired by a late and impromptu entry for a Coarse Acting competition produced by my old friend Mr Geoff Webb, who recommends that the entire cast should be drunk, as in the original show. Its place in this volume is to demonstrate that *all* opera is Coarse. *All's Well That Ends As You Like It* has been written (believe it or not) by public demand. The last chapter of *The Art of Coarse Acting* consists of an all-purpose Coarse Elizabethan historical play entitled *'Tis Pity She's The Merry Wife of Henry IV, Part One*, which enabled a Coarse Actor to play several different parts, all of increasing moronity. It is another sign of a Coarse Actor that he is never allowed merely to play one part but spends his time dashing from role to role as messenger, lord, assistant clown, soldier and so forth. Many people asked if I would write another Coarse play with Shakespearean overtones, so this time I have written a comedy, with similar opportunities for some bold individual to play five parts. In true Elizabethan style, this comedy is totally unfunny. The four plays can be put together to form a full-length show, as at Edinburgh. I have included some of the alterations introduced for *The Coarse Acting Show* but I hope other directors won't hesitate to introduce their own ideas.

Finally, thanks to so many people, friends and strangers, whose acting has helped to provide material for this volume.

Michael Green.

Michael Green has laid down rules for the holding of Coarse Acting Festivals and anyone wishing to hold such a Festival should apply to Curtis Brown Limited, 1 Craven Hill, London W2 3EP, for a performing licence and a set of rules.

IL FORNICAZIONE

IL FORNICAZIONE

(The Adulterer)

An Opera in One Act
By Michael Green

From an idea by Geoffrey Webb and Kevin Fells
pirated from Shostokovitch

First produced as part of *The Coarse Acting Show* at
the Cathedral Hall, Edinburgh, on August 22nd, 1977,
with the following cast:

A Triangle Player	Lorna Duval
A Conductor	Michael Green
The Countess Formaggio	Ann Johnson
Maid	Sonia Pearson
Alfonso, lover to the Countess	David Crewes
The Count Formaggio, elderly husband to the Countess	David Pearson
Attendants, Huntsmen, etc.	Michael Langridge
	John Turner
	Richard Gaunt
	Robin Duval
	Richard Johnson
	Peter Macnamara

A dead stag

PRODUCTION NOTES

It need hardly be said that in producing this, it is necessary to over-stress the normal operatic conventions. As stated in the stage directions, it is intended that the players should sing in *recitative*, which for those who don't know is a sort of musical declamation used for the mundane dialogue of an opera, as distinct from the "songs" and the tuneful bits. It tends to be on one or two notes only, like this:

But of course, anyone who can make up their own tunes to the non-dialogue pieces, such as the huntsmen's song and Alfonso's little solos, is welcome to do so.

Incidentally, it is perfectly possible to perform the piece without the conductor or triangle player, omitting the sub-plot about the lost orchestra and plunging straight in.

IL FORNICAZIONE

Before the CURTAIN *rises a Triangle Player, carrying her apparatus, enters the empty orchestra pit and settles herself. The Conductor then enters and, after tapping his baton for silence, addresses the audience*

Conductor Ladies and gentlemen, I regret to have to tell you an unfortunate accident has occurred. Our talented operatic section had hoped tonight to render an excerpt from that great masterpiece *Il Fornicazione*— "The Adulterer". Unfortunately, the van containing the orchestra broke down on the way and the only members of the music section to arrive are myself, your conductor, and Miss Cartwright, our Lady Triangle, who came by bicycle. The cast have sportingly agreed, however, to sing unaccompanied, except by myself and Miss Cartwright our Lady Triangle. But we ask your indulgence in case the performance is not up to our usual high standard. Thank you.

He turns to the "orchestra" and taps with his baton for silence. He then vigorously launches into what we may presume is the overture, calling in non-existent musicians and urging the absent orchestra to supreme heights. Suddenly, in the middle of a particularly energetic spasm, he points dramatically at the triangle player, who gives one solitary "ping". After a few moments the CURTAIN *rises on an interior setting of unsurpassed grandeur, the home of the Countess Formaggio. The Countess is seated, sewing, accompanied by her maid. In the absence of any sound from the orchestra all characters should sing in recitative or invent their own opera-type music or indeed do anything they like. The main point is to bellow as loudly as possible*

Countess Ah! I am weary. Yes, weary. How weary I am. Weary. Weary. Ah, weary.
Maid She is weary. My mistress is weary.
Countess Very weary.
Maid My mistress is very weary.
Countess (*rising and pacing around*) Where is my young lover, Alfonso? He should be here by now. My elderly and doting husband, the Count Formaggio, is out hunting and I have arranged a tryst with Alfonso. But he is not here. O, where is he? (*She looks out of the window and gives a shriek*) Ah! He is here. He comes.
Maid He comes.

Alfonso stands at the window

Alfonso My love, it is I, Alfonso.
My heart is beating with love for you.

I flew here on the wings of passion
But even they were too slow.

He tries to get through the window. As he is very fat he does this with some difficulty. He then leaps heavily to the floor with a crash

Maria! My little one!

The Countess weighs about sixteen stone. He seizes her violently

Countess Alfonso!
Alfonso Ah! It is the rose of my heart.
        Let me press it to my bosom.
        Surely no rose ever smelt like this?
        I have plucked it from a garden,
        The sweetest on earth,
        Surely the garden of Cupid.
Countess Alfonso!
Alfonso Yes, beloved?
Countess Will you take some refreshment?
Alfonso A little wine, please.
Countess Red or white?
Alfonso Rosé. Slightly chilled. With one-third water.
Countess To love, which conquers all!
Alfonso To my loved one!

They pledge each other and drink greedily

Countess This wine is like fire! Behold how greedily it courses through my veins!
Maid Behold how greedily it courses through her veins.
Alfonso Yes, wine is the elixir of love. Let us drink to Cupid. Ha!

They drain their papier-mâché goblets and hurl them over their shoulders where the Maid just manages to dodge them

Alfonso (*bursting into song*) Sparkling wine!
Countess   Drink divine!
Alfonso   Of love the sign
Countess   That makes you mine!
Alfonso Ha, ha, ha!
Countess Ha, ha, ha! But hark!

A stirring is seen in the orchestra and the Triangle Player strikes five times under the baton of the Conductor

The Triangle Player then gets up and leaves

'Tis five o'clock! You must not tarry longer, beloved. My elderly and doting husband is out hunting, but I expect to hear his horn at any moment announcing his return from the chase.

Alfonso A few moments snatched from misery.
       I live only for your smile.
       Yet I see it so rarely.
       So rarely. Alas, so rarely.

Maid He sees it but rarely.

Countess Alas, 'tis true.

Alfonso It cannot continue!

Countess What do you mean?

Alfonso If I cannot possess you for myself
       I shall die.

Countess Ah!

Maid He will die.

Alfonso Yes, you must be mine and mine alone.

Countess But what about my elderly and doting husband?

Alfonso I shall challenge him to a duel. One of us must die.

He raises his dagger high. The Countess gives a shout of alarm and drags down his arm with such violence that he plunges the dagger into his groin. He gives a cry of pain and a strange expression appears on his face

Countess No, beloved, his men would secretly murder you. I have a better
    plan. I have here a vial of deadly poison . . .

Alfonso (*in a squeaky voice*) Poison!

Maid Poison!

Countess Yes, poison. It was given to me by an old witch in the mountains.
    (*She drags a vial from her bosom with difficulty*) Listen, when my husband
    returns from hunting he will be hungry. I have prepared a mushroom
    pie. I shall put the poison in the pie and he will trouble us no more.

Alfonso And we shall be together for ever!

Countess For ever!

Maid For ever!

Alfonso For ever,
       And ever,
       And ever,
       And ever!

Countess And ever,
       And ever,
       And ever,
       And ever,
       And ever!

Maid And ever.

Alfonso No! It troubles me! There is a pain about my heart. (*He clutches
    his abdomen*) We must not kill your husband. To do so would be
    wrong in the eyes of heaven, and very dangerous as well.

Countess But, beloved—hark!

The sound of a hunting-horn is heard

    'Tis he. My elderly and doting husband returns. You must hide. Quick,
    in here.

Alfonso No, I wish to meet him face to face.
Countess He has two hundred followers. They will surely kill you.
Alfonso I go.

The Countess drags him to a door and pushes him through it

Maid Make haste, my master is coming with his hunting party.

The horn sounds louder

Alfonso opens the door

Alfonso My hat!

The Countess gives it to him and pushes him back

The Countess and the Maid then compose themselves as if nothing had happened. Outside there is a very loud blast on the horn and a tremendous noise of baying and howling

The Count Formaggio enters with about 200 attendants, roistering and dragging a dead stag behind them

Omnes Sing ho! for the hunt, the jolly old hunt.
The hunters are men for the women and wine.
We hunt all the boars and we kill all the stags
For hunting of sports is the finest of fine.
Of fine, of fine, of fine.
Yes, hunting of sports is the finest of fine.
Hooray! Ha, ha, ha, ha!

The Huntsmen break into jolly cries of "rhubarb"

Count Ah, dearest wife, I have returned——

He is interrupted by the Huntsmen, etc., who suddenly burst into their chorus. Indeed, they can do this as often as they like

Omnes Sing ho! for the hunt, the jolly old hunt
The hunters are men for the women and wine!
Hooray! Ha, ha, ha, ha! (etc.)

More cries of "rhubarb"

Count (*looking a trifle peeved at this interruption*) I have returned. How hungry I am after hunting all day.
Countess Would you like a mushroom pie?
Count I would like nothing better.
Countess I will fetch it.

The Countess exits, fondling her vial meaningly

Count How weary I am. But how fortunate that I have a lovely young wife who looks after me as I grow old. If she were to be unfaithful I would die.

Omnes If she were to be unfaithful he would die.

The Countess enters, bearing a sinister-looking pie, giving off an evil steam, probably green

Countess Behold, here is the mushroom pie.

Count Ah! I like nothing better than a mushroom pie, unless it is two mushroom pies.

Omnes Ha, ha, ha, ha! (*They drink and hurl wine goblets maniacally all over the stage*)

The Count sits down and starts to eat. A cloud of vile-looking gas arises

Maid Sir, I cannot stand idly by and see you meet a terrible death. Do not eat it, it is poisoned!

Omnes Poisoned?

Maid Yes, poisoned. With a deadly nectar which is tasteless.

Omnes Do not eat it, it is poisoned; do not eat it, it is poisoned; do not eat it, it is poisoned . . . (*They can go on like this as long as they like*)

Count Poisoned? And by whom—my loving wife? What a joke! Ha, ha, ha, ha!

Omnes Ha, ha, ha, ha!

The Count eats voraciously. Suddenly he rises and staggers

Count Aaaaaaaaaaaaaaaaaaaaaaah. It *is* poisoned. I die.

Omnes It was poisoned, it was poisoned, it was poisoned . . ., etc. (*Repeated a great many times to one another*)

Countess Yes, I poisoned your pie with the contents of a secret vial which I concealed about my person and which was given to me by an old witch in the mountains.

Omnes She poisoned his pie with the contents of a secret vial which she concealed about her person and which was given to her by an old witch in the mountains.

Meanwhile, the Count totters around a good deal, clutching himself

Ah! He falls.

Count Why have you done this to me? Have I wronged you in some way?

Countess I wish to be free to be with my lover. It was for his sake that I poisoned the pie.

Omnes For her lover, for her lover, for her lover.

Count A lover! Aaaaaaaah! My life is ebbing. I feel the heavy hand of death upon my nostrils. Yet I forgive you, my love.

Omnes He forgives her, he forgives her, he forgives her.

Countess Alas! What have I done?

Omnes You have poisoned him.

Count I die. (*He lies down and drums his heels, then raises himself on one elbow*) Grant me one request. Let me see your lover ere I die.

Countess Never!

Omnes Yes! Bring him hither!

Countess No!

Count Yes, I wish it.

Countess Very well. Alfonso!

Count Alfonso! Can it be?

Alfonso enters. He sees the Count and stares, horrified

Alfonso!

Alfonso Father!

The Count and Alfonso embrace. Everyone registers horror

Count Alas, my long-lost son Alfonso, the child of my first marriage! He was believed to have been carried away by gypsies and the shock caused the death of his mother. And now he is my second wife's lover! What a scurvy knave is Fate! Alas, I feel once more the heavy hand of death upon my nostrils—I—die. (*He sinks back*)

Alfonso Father! Forgive me!

Count (*raising himself*) My son, she is to blame, that young wife of mine.

Omnes Yes, she is to blame, that young wife of his, she is to blame. To blame. To blame. To blame.

Count I die cursing her. (*He sinks back*)

Alfonso Vile woman, you have killed my father! But you shall not live to triumph! (*He draws a pistol and tries to shoot the Countess but the gun will not fire. Undeterred, he seizes his dagger and stabs her. Just as he is about to do so the sound of a shot rings out*)

Countess Aaaaah! I die. (*She staggers and falls*)

Alfonso Ring down the curtain.
          The comedy is over.
          Money will be returned at the Great Box Office of Heaven.
          Farewell, cruel world.
          Never again will you be able to wound me
          With your knavish tricks.
          Farewell.

He goes to stab himself, but changes his mind

          No! I shall share my father's fate!

He cuts himself a generous portion of pie, sprinkles some salt on it, and eats it. After a moment he falls writhing

Ah!

Omnes He has poisoned himself also. O, horrid sight. (*They all sob*)

Alfonso Ugh!

Count Ouch!

Countess Ah!

Alfonso Oh!
Countess Eek!
Count Aaaaaah!

They writhe around a bit. During the following exchange all three suddenly recover their full vigour, singing and waving their arms as if full of life

Countess (*raising herself*) Farewell, beloved husband and lover. I die blessing you both.
Alfonso (*standing up*) We are but playthings of Fate.
Count We are but pawns.
Countess As on a chessboard, no less.
Count Farewell, son and wife. The cruel hand of Death is on my nostrils. I go, I die. Farewell. Aaaaaaaaaaaaaaah! (*He drums his heels and dies*)
Omnes He goes. He says farewell, he says farewell, he says farewell.
Countess I cannot hold in life any more. Death, I welcome thee! Aaaaaaah! (*She dies somewhat extravagantly*)
Omnes Behold, she dies.
Alfonso I come to join you both. I die, I die, I die, I die. (*He sinks a little lower each time and dies*)
Omnes They die. They are dying. They are dead.
Maid Some of you carry my master to the chapel.

Four of the crowd detach themselves for this task while the others begin a solemn dirge

Omnes It was the mushrooms. They were poisoned. It was the mushrooms. They were poisoned, etc., etc. (*Ad nauseam*)

Unfortunately the bearers have difficulty with the Count. They hoist him with some trouble on their shoulders in the manner of Hamlet but he slips off. Eventually they get him back and start to lurch off-stage but discover they are going in the wrong direction. In the subsequent about-turn the Count is roughly treated and cries out in distress. They lurch into the wings where there is a hideous crash. The CURTAIN *falls. The maid, Alfonso, Count and Countess take a bow. Bouquets are presented. That of the Maid is bigger than that of the Countess, who snatches it from the Maid*

CURTAIN

STREUTH

STREUTH

An original whodunit, as performed by
the East Loathing Amateur Dramatic Society

By David Pearson, Michael Langridge, John Turner,
Richard Gaunt, Margaret Turner, John Wilbourn,
David Crewes, Lorna Duval, Sonia Pearson and others
unknown

First produced at the Questors Theatre, Ealing, London,
in November 1972, with the following cast of characters:

The Inspector	David Pearson
Mr Oliver D'Arcy	Richard Gaunt
Mrs D'Arcy	Margaret Turner
Hubert D'Arcy	John Wilbourn
The Major	John Turner
The Vicar	David Crewes
James	Michael Langridge
Cook	Lorna Duval
Prompt	Sonia Pearson
Sergeant	Michael Green

The play was directed by anyone who happened to be
passing at the time

STREUTH
List of Characters

Inspector: It should be remembered that all police Inspectors, as portrayed by Coarse actors, come from solid Yorkshire mining stock. For make-up, refer to the All Purpose Character Chart shown in Chapter 2 of *The Art of Coarse Acting*. Stock walk no. 5 (tread like an elephant in diving boots). Keep hat on at all time indoors.

The Inspector in real life probably thinks of himself as the society's figurehead, the one who pulls everything together at the eleventh hour. In fact, the image that he presents to the audience will be that of Damocles on a bad day.

Mr D'Arcy: This middle-aged part should be played by someone in their early twenties, as an obvious exercise in miscasting. Due to his evident youth, the make-up is a grotesque assortment of lines.

Mrs D'Arcy: She merely got the part because she was the only one with a front room large enough to rehearse in. Since she can't disguise her "common" accent, she ought to be playing the part of the Cook, but demanded something better.

Hubert (their son): This part (if at all possible) should be played by the father of the actor playing Mr D'Arcy. He remains motionless throughout the play and stares with fixed gaze at the audience, rocking on his heels. He speaks as if hypnotised and reads most of his lines from a crib inside a cigarette case.

The Major: His concept of a Major is based on something he saw in a Hollywood film. Thus he wears a monocle—which nearly blinds him—and sprinkles his lines with extra exclamations such as "By jove!" and "What?".

The Corpse (Henry): Normally, this will be played by a dummy, but if any member of the company is brave enough to play the part, he should have a heavy cold which will enable him to sneeze at the wrong moment.

James: Modelled on Quasimodo, both in make-up and stance (see *The Art of Coarse Acting*, Chapter 2, "Warts"). Speaks something like Bernard Miles as Long John Silver. A one-character man and this is it.

The Cook: Very little is known about the Cook, since she spends most of the play with her cap rammed down over her eyes. A refined, middle-class lady, she speaks with a ghastly attempt at being working-class. Ought to be playing Mrs D'Arcy.

The Vicar (Rupert): The archetypal villain of melodrama, with rolling eyes and black beard. Is inclined to mouth other people's speeches, especially when staring closely at their faces.

Sergeant: Although the actor playing this part has been cast in twenty plays, he has yet to appear on stage. At the point of his entrance, he will be in the pub next door.

Prompt: This personage is listed under the Cast as she will form an important part of the performance of the play. At moments of stress it may even be necessary for her to appear in order to make her point to the actors. At the very least, her hand, waving a script, should be seen to appear round the edge of the scenery.

ACT I

SCENE 1

The drawing-room of the D'Arcy Manor. The house lights are dim

Music: "Mars" from The Planets *by Holst (the bit at the end which bashes on interminably)*

Above the music the Cast can be heard getting into position, falling over the furniture, swearing, shushing, etc. Then there is a pregnant hiatus, while the music grinds on. Eventually, the Stage Manager remembers to raise the CURTAIN, *revealing the Inspector, Mr and Mrs D'Arcy, the Major and Hubert grouped motionless around a settee and staring desperately at the audience. A shroud of cigar smoke envelopes the Major. The Inspector prepares to speak, but is suddenly transfixed by the vacant area of stage in front of his feet. He quivers, blinks and looks nervously into the wings*

The CURTAIN *comes down. "Mars" resurfaces, comes to an end and is followed by a snatch of something totally inappropriate*

The CURTAIN *rises again. The vacant space at the Inspector's feet is now occupied by a dummy with a huge poker protruding from its chest. If the corpse is a live actor, he should clasp the murder weapon*

Inspector Now. Will you be good enough to identify the deceased, please.
D'Arcy (*peering at the corpse, registering shock*) My brother, actually. Henry.
Mrs D'Arcy (*over the top*) Poor, dear 'Enery. I just can't believe it!
D'Arcy Really, Inspector, can't this interrogation wait . . . ?

The actor who plays D'Arcy regards his lines as something to be got rid of as soon as possible. The preceding line should therefore be delivered as "Really, Inspectorcan'tthisinterrogationwait?"

Inspector (*taken aback*) Er . . .
   (*Recovering quickly*) Afraid not, sir. Perhaps you would be good enough to tell me where you all were when the murder was committed.
D'Arcy Well,Inspector,Iwasinthedining-room,finishingoffapieceofCamembertwhenIheardthis—(*breath*)—screamaterriblescreamfollowedbya dullthudIrushedoutintothehallandIhappenedtonoticethatthegrandfatherclocksaidfivetonine . . .
Mrs D'Arcy Oh, no, Olivah, I was in the kitchen giving Cook tomorrer's meenu and the nine o'clock news was on the wireless.
Hubert No . . . Mater . . . That . . . can't be right. (*He dries and pulls out a cigarette case with the lines inside*) . . . I was . . . in . . . the . . . Library . . . reading . . . Buckle's *History of Civilization* . . . when . . . I . . . heard

... a ... scream ... (*He dries again and changes to another cigarette case*) ... automatically ... looked ... at ... my ... wrist ... watch ... and ... noticed ... that ... the ... time ... was ... seven ... thirty-five ...

At this point, Hubert utilizes a traditional corny joke, by looking at his wristwatch and pouring the contents of his glass into Mrs D'Arcy's lap

Inspector Hmm—there seems to be a discrepancy here. This is most suspicious—I wonder what the explanation could be.

A pause

Major Seems pretty obvious to me, Inspector, by Jove, by Jove!
Inspector Does it, sir?
Major Yes—er—ah! I would surmise that his wristwatch—(*he indicates D'Arcy Senior*)—and his grandfather clock—(*he indicates D'Arcy Junior*)—were both wrong.
Inspector I believe, sir, you have hit upon the solution, sir. (*He goes to raise his hand, index finger pointing to the skies, in an "aha" position, only to find his hand is stuck in the lining of his raincoat. After a struggle, he manages to free it and strikes the pose*) And what were you doing while this was going on?

A pause

Major Who, me?
Inspector (*laughing nervously*) Yes, sir, *YOU!*
Major Oh ... (*He asks the next line as if it were a question*) I was taking a breath of fresh air in the garden, Inspector?
Inspector (*sighing relievedly*) I see, sir, did *you* hear the scream?
Major No, Inspector, can't say I did, though I did see something deucedly funny.
Inspector (*with venom*) Oh, and what was that?
Major A figure, Inspector, at the drawing-room window, wearing evening dress.
Inspector Was it the deceased, sir?
Major No, Inspector, don't think it was. It was a broad-shouldered chappy with a long black beard.
Inspector Could it have been either of these two gentlemen, here?
Major It's so damned difficult to tell. The moment I caught sight of him, the damned light went orff.
Inspector (*raising his finger*) That would imply there was someone else in the room at the time?
Major By Jove, Inspector, you're right! By Jove!

The Major, having finished his lines at last, resumes his inane grin

D'Arcy Lookhere,Inspector,we'veallexplainedthatwewerenowherenearthe sceneofthecrimeatthetime ...

A pause

Inspector Was anyone else present in the house?

D'Arcy OnlythecookandJamesthebutler . . .

Mrs D'Arcy Yes, Inspector, James found pore dear 'Enery here and reported the matter t'me.

Inspector In that case, madam, I think that I had better have a word with both of them.

Mrs D'Arcy I will ring for them, Hinspector. (*She does not*)

Inspector Can you think of any reason why anyone should want to kill your bruvver—er—brother, Mr D'Arcy?

D'Arcy SofarasIknowmybrotherhadnoenemiesintheworldapartfromour step—(*breath*)—brotherRupertWhodisappearedonanexpeditiontoPatagoniatenyearsago . . .

Inspector (*to the audience*) *RUPERT*, you say?

D'Arcy Yes,Inspector—(*to the audience*)—*RUPERT*.

Mrs D'Arcy But otherwise he was loved by horl.

Hubert (*reading from his cigarette case*) And . . . he . . . was . . . a . . . National . . . Hunt . . . jockey.

Inspector Well, someone had reason to dislike him, and this—(*pointing a finger*)—is what I intend to find out this evening.

D'Arcy Ah, James!

All the Cast members look up R

The Cook appears up R *at the same time as James arrives up* L. *They both realize there is a mistake and withdraw. The figures of James and the Cook cross behind the french windows. Pause. The Cook crosses back, following James. James and the Cook arrive* R

The Cast, by this time, have all turned up L

James You rang, zur?

Everybody on stage turns to face the wayward pair

D'Arcy Ahhh!Comein,James,nowIdon'twantyoutoworry,theInspectorhere wantstoaskyouafewsimplequestions.

Inspector Thank you, Mr D'Arcy. Now, James, I believe that you discovered the body.

James That'z roight, zur. I wuz on moy way to the drawring-room to make up the foir when Oi urd this ere scream. I ran in ere. (*Pause. He points to the exact point on the carpet that he ran in to. He moves up stage, to dominate the better*)

The Lights go down to a single Spot, just slightly missing James, but—experienced that he is—he moves into it

The room wuz in blackness. Moonlight wuz shoining through the French windows, which I built myself—(*a reference to the fact that he didn't get a mention in the programme for this feat. He pauses for effect*)—suddenly, a man ran through the windows and disappeared into the

garden. I switched on the loight and saw Mr D'Arcy loying there—
DEAD!!!

The Lights return to normal

Inspector You obviously disturbed the murderer before he found what he
was looking for.

James (*sarcastically*) With my limited knowledge of criminology, sir, I
think you could say that. (*He tuts and withdraws*)

D'Arcy (*sensing a storm brewing because it was the Inspector who proof-
read the stencil for the programme, jumps in hurriedly*) Whatd'yousup-
posehewaslookingfor,Inspector?

Inspector (*close to hysteria*) I don't know yet, Mr D'Arcy. What happened
then?

James Everybody came rushing in. Mr Oliver told someone to ring the—
huh—police.

Inspector I see.

D'Arcy Thereyouare,Inspector,themurderercameinthroughtheFrenchwin-
dowsmurderedpoorHenryandrushedoutthewayhehadcome.

Inspector (*once again trying to raise his index finger in a stance position
and once again finding it stuck in the trenchcoat pocket*) Not necessarily,
Mr D'Arcy!

D'Arcy Whatdoyoumean,Inspector?

Inspector I observe these windows have not been forced from the outside
and that there is a catch of intricate design, the working of which would
be understood only by members of the immediate household. (*He moves
to the entrance down* R, *stumbling over the corpse en route*) The light
switch is here by this door. The murderer probably came in this way,
turned off the light like this . . . (*He switches off the light switch. The
Lights stay on*) Like this . . .

The Lights stay on—pause—the Lights go off

. . . murdered Henry and made his escape through the french windows . . . (*Reconstructing the crime, he crosses to the french windows, en
route accidentally stepping on the Major's toe, banging his knee on the
settee and poking Mrs D'Arcy with his ball-point pen*) I'll just put the
lights on again. (*Crossing back to the light switch, he falls headlong over
the corpse*)

*The Lights come on immediately, revealing the Inspector lying full-length
along the corpse, but reaching out towards the distant light switch in a
gallant effort to preserve the illusion. Acknowledging defeat, the Inspector
rises and stares down at the corpse with undisguised loathing*

Let's get the corpse out of the way, shall we?

*The other characters are momentarily non-plussed by this improvisation,
so the Inspector takes hold of the corpse, lifts it up, swings it round and
deposits it on the settee. He does not notice that the head has been left
behind on the floor. Hubert does. He quivers slightly, then puts his foot*

*over the head, and back-heels it to D'Arcy, who is standing beside him.
D'Arcy picks it up and passes it sideways to Mrs D'Arcy. Mrs D'Arcy
picks it up and passes it sideways to the Major. The Major reunites the head
with its body*

Mrs D'Arcy But surely, Inspector, you don't suspect any of us?
Inspector At this stage, Madam, I have to inspect everyone.

*The Cook, who has been dreaming of blissful nights in Portofino, surfaces
slowly from her trance*

Cook Mr D'Arcy . . .
D'Arcy Yes, Eliza?
Cook I really think I ought to say summat.
Inspector Yes, miss?

The Cook steps forward two paces

Cook Well, sir, it was like this 'ere. This afternoon, about half-past four,
there was this man standing by the gate—Gawd love us! Funny looking
gentleman he was. With a beard. A great black beard. He was just
standing there, looking. Fair gimme the creeps it did.
Inspector Did you mention it to anyone?
Cook I didn't think any more of it, to tell the truth. Cor lumme. I wasn't
to know anything like this was going to happen. (*She steps back*)
Mrs D'Arcy Come now, Eliza. Don't upset yourself.
Inspector Thank you, miss. That could be important.

*The Inspector turns to look at the corpse and notices, apparently for the
first time, the poker buried in its chest. He recoils a few steps*

Ha! Looks like we've found the murder weapon. Sergeant! Take it
down to the lab and have it fingerprinted.

*It takes a couple of seconds for the Cast to realize that the Sergeant is not
among them—indeed, that no-one has seen him around that evening. The
full horror of the situation begins to dawn on them*

Inspector (*bellowing off*) SERGEANT!
Prompt (*off*) Very good, Sir.

*The Inspector glares at the Prompt. He decides to carry on and see what
happens*

Inspector Use your handkerchief, Sergeant—we don't want . . .

*The Inspector realizes the futility of that approach. After a moment's thought
he pulls out his handkerchief, withdraws the poker from the body with his
other hand and then places it in the handkerchief. Having got this far, his
inspiration deserts him. He stares at the poker. The rest of the Cast are
transfixed. Suddenly, the Inspector thrusts the poker back into the corpse*

Right. Well, we'll take that down to the lab after we have finished this—
interrogation.

The Inspector blows his nose into the handkerchief. There is a long pause.
The Cast are completely lost. The Inspector snaps his fingers at the Prompt.
The Prompt is also lost

The Prompt appears round the edge of the scenery

Prompt I don't know where we are.
Inspector (*assuming this to be his cue*) I don't know where we are.
Prompt "Would you like a drink?"

This line sounds familiar to each one of a now highly strung Cast

The Prompt disappears behind the scenery

All "Would you like a drink?"
Mrs D'Arcy (*whose line it actually is*) Would you like a drink, Inspector?
Inspector (*with relief*) No thank you, madam, I never drink while I'm on
duty.

This is the cue for the Vicar's entrance. He appears at the french windows,
his arms full of old clothing, which completely obscures his face. He tries
to open the french windows, but is not aware that a stage-hand, for reasons
understandable only to another stage-hand, nailed them to the floor that
afternoon. He rattles the doors and the set shakes in sympathy

The Cast covers the hiatus by improvisation. They queue up for drinks and
walk around, bumping each other and sneaking glances at the french win-
dows. The Inspector carries on bravely

No, I never drink when I'm on duty. It's not allowed. Drinking on
duty. Against the rules. You might say. Ho, ho, etc.

The Vicar finally gives up at the french windows and disappears. After a
brief pause, he enters through the fireplace

Vicar Good evening.
D'Arcy Goodevening,Vicar.Niceofyoutocall.
Mrs D'Arcy But what happened to the Reverend Courage?
Vicar What?
Mrs D'Arcy Reverend Courage of St Stephen's. He's our vicar.
Vicar Oh, he's sick. I am the new replacement.

The Inspector decides to take matters into his own hands. He takes the
bundle of clothing from the Vicar

Inspector Look, sir. Why don't we get rid of these bits and pieces for
you. Put them down here. (*He drops the clothing on the sofa, on top of
the corpse*) May I ask what you are doing here, Vicar?

Vicar Just collecting for our sale of work.
Mrs D'Arcy Oh, we thought you'd come round because of poor dear Henry.

A scenery flat teeters. James rushes to it and leans against it for the rest of the play

Inspector May I ask, sir, whether you have ever been to this house before?
Vicar No, never, I'm ashamed to say.
Inspector Are you sure of that, sir?
Vicar Absolutely positive, Inspector.
Inspector In that case, sir, how do you explain . . .

Pause. The telephone bell rings. This obviously startles the Cast

Mrs D'Arcy Answer the doorbell, James.
Inspector That will be the ambulance.
Mrs D'Arcy Let them in, James.

James runs to do so, but the flat starts to fall and he hastily has to resume his position

James (*improvising*) Moi old wound is troubling me, sir. Eliza can let them in.

Eliza is dreaming again

Hubert Yes, Eliza, go on. Hurry along.
Cook (*waking up*) What? Oh, definitely. Right-ho.

Cook exits

Vicar Well, if you will excuse me, Inspector, I really must get on my rounds. (*He tries to tear the Will from the corpse's hand, but it will not come, so he removes the whole arm*) It really is delightful meeting you all . . .
Inspector Just a moment, sir, not so fast.
Vicar Yes, Inspector?
Hubert (*reading from his cigarette case*) The Inspector is on to something.
Mrs D'Arcy Be quiet, Hubert.
D'Arcy LettheInspectorfinish.
Inspector I think you're hiding something.
Vicar I have nothing to hide, Inspector.
Inspector Then perhaps you'd answer this question. If you have never been to this house before, how did you manage to come into the room so easily through those french windows—which have a lock of intricate design, known only to immediate members of this household?

A dramatic pause

Vicar All right, Inspector, you win! (*He tears off his false beard, revealing a real beard underneath*)
All Rupert!

Vicar Yes, Rupert. And now I have the document that I came for—
  (*brandishing the Will*)—I wish you all good night. (*He turns to go*)
Inspector Just a moment, sir, not so fast.
Vicar Yes, Inspector?
Hubert The Inspector is on to something.
Mrs D'Arcy Be quiet, Hubert.
D'Arcy LettheInspectorfinish.

The Vicar tries to put the false beard back on and return the arm

Inspector I think you are hiding something.
Vicar I've nothing to hide, Inspector.
Inspector (*after a pause, speaking in a strange monotone*) Then perhaps
  you'd answer this question. If you have never been to this house before
  how did you manage to come into this room so easily through those
  french windows which have a lock of intricate design known only to
  the immediate members of the household?
Vicar All right, Inspector, you win! (*He removes the beard*)
All (*dispiritedly*) Rupert.
Vicar Yes, Rupert. (*Brandishing the Will*) And now I have found the
  document I came for . . .
Inspector Just a moment, sir, not so fast.
Vicar Yes, Inspector?
Hubert (*still blandly unaware*) The Inspector is on to something.

*The Inspector snatches the cigarette case from him and hurls it into the
wings*

Mrs D'Arcy Be quiet, Hubert!
D'Arcy LettheInspectorfinish . . .

From this point, the CURTAIN *may mercifully be drawn at the discretion of
the stage manager. The audience leaving the theatre may still catch the
occasional familiar phrase as the play continues on its inexorable course, or
the collapse of the teetering flat might signal the end*

A COLLIER'S TUESDAY TEA

A COLLIER'S TUESDAY TEA

A Mining Epic

By Richard Gaunt, Michael Langridge, David Pearson, John Turner, Lorna Duval, David Crewes, Sonia Pearson, Margaret Turner and John Wilbourn, etc.

First produced at the Questors Theatre, Ealing, London, in 1975, with the following cast of characters:

Ida Hepplethwaite	Lorna Duval
Daniel Obadiah Hepplethwaite	David Crewes
Victoria Hepplethwaite	Sonia Pearson
Albert Hepplethwaite	Richard Gaunt
Joe Clegghorn	David Pearson
Margery Hackforth	Margaret Turner
Lionel Headbracket	John Wilbourn
P.C. Clement Boothroyd	John Turner
Jed Throttle	Michael Langridge

PRODUCTION NOTES

As the so-called script of this epic already consists largely of stage directions, I felt it would be better to put some production advice in the form of notes rather than overload the already heavily burdened text. Obviously, there is scope for a lot of flexibility in producing this piece. For instance, it may be possible to obtain a wheelchair which can be adapted so a wheel falls off and is replaced on stage. Or perhaps Grandpa could get his scarf caught in the spokes and nearly strangle himself?

It must be remembered that the table is the focus of the play. It should be very large, which makes the business of the actors having to support it, much more effective. As regards the legs, it is absolutely essential that they are not connected to the table-top at all. The table-top should just rest on them so that when the time comes for their removal they will fall down easily and spectacularly. In the Questors' production, the legs consisted of stout cardboard tubes used as the cores of large reels of paper. But there is no reason why they should not be wood, as long as they are heavy enough to fall with a good thud. And it must be plain to the audience that the Cast are supporting the table.

The food on the table is another important item. It must not merely *be* inedible. It must *look* inedible as well. It really must look utterly and completely phoney. The Bunny Langridge Players had a brilliant idea—they constructed a huge cake and a cheese from polystyrene. When attempts were made to cut these, they broke into vast fragments. Another ingenious device was the use of slices of bread made from plastic and plasticine sausages which drooped obscenely when lifted up. But leave some genuine stale buns for Vicky to get gummed up on.

Tea figures frequently in the script. As one of the signs of a Coarse production is that there is never enough of any property liquid, whether it be tea or whisky, I feel it best to have the teapot completely empty, but with Ida spraying imaginary tea in all directions. As she knows the pot is empty she does not bother to pay attention to what she is doing and says her lines through the business with the result that if there *had* been any tea in the pot she would have poured about three pints on the tablecloth or over the family.

Dan might well be one of those actors with a wobbling accent. He could start off Yorkshire and end up Scottish. Grandpa is another important character, since the audience will undoubtedly be watching him much of the time. It is important that he is utterly incompetent at controlling his wheelchair.

When this play was produced as part of The Coarse Acting Show at Edinburgh we inserted the extra line "moonlight was shining through the French windows" in Jed's speech at the end, after ". . . it were terrible." This was because the actor playing Jed had also played James, the butler, in "Streuth", and we reckoned he was the sort who would mix up the lines of one play with another. He would stop in embarrassment as he realized what he had done.

But more important than gimmickry in this piece is complete and utter sincerity. The humour comes from the contrast between the grimness the play is trying to portray and the lunacy of the events which overcome this earnest production. The more genuinely sincere the acting the greater the contrast and the funnier the result.

Incidentally, in case a translation is needed of Vicky's incoherent outburst on page 36, here it is:

1. "Be nice to him, Father, I beg you . . ."
2. "But Father! How can you do this to me?"
3. "I do. No-one understands my feelings at all. I am a woman, a real woman. My feelings are like everybody else's feelings. Oh I hate you all! You won't let me lead my own life!"

One more point: make sure any tablecloth does not prevent the legs falling cleanly.

A COLLIER'S TUESDAY TEA

(with apologies to D. H. Lawrence)

CHARACTERS

Ida Hepplethwaite (Matriarch of the Hepplethwaite Clan)
Daniel Obadiah Hepplethwaite (her spouse)
Victoria Hepplethwaite (their daughter)
Albert Hepplethwaite (their son)
Joe Clegghorn (Grandfather)
Margery Hackforth (a neighbour)
Lionel Headbracket (Victoria's sweetheart)
P.C. Clement Boothroyd (a policeman?)
Jed Throttle (a relation of the Hepplethwaite family)

The Scene is the sparse but cosy cottage of the Hepplethwaite family in Slagton, a mining village. Dominating the room is a large table set for high tea. Over in a corner is a stove, glowing warmly. The Lights fade up. Grim music

It is evening and Ida Hepplethwaite and Margery Hackforth are discovered (in the wrong positions). Grandpa Joe Clegghorn enters in a wheelchair. He has been pushed from offstage with great force towards the front of the stage. He screeches to a halt barely three inches from eternity. There is a pause. No-one is certain of what has happened. The Cast find their correct positions. The music stops. The Lights start to fade but think better of it

The sound of a violent thunderstorm is heard, frightening the Cast and the lighting man. All twitch and then relax again. Grandpa cackles

Ida Tea?

Margery Please. (*Pause*) I see your Albert's walking out with the Ackroyd girl, then.

Ida Well, what's wrong with that? (*She tries to cut some bread and breaks the knife, so has to tear off a piece*)

Margery Oh, nothing, only folks is saying that he's got ideas above his station, that's all.

Ida I don't see any harm in it, and besides, he's old enough to know his own mind, and I happen to know that right now there's something more important than Lucy Ackroyd uppermost in his thoughts.

Margery Oh?

Ida gives Margery an empty tea-cup. At the same time there is a fearful crash off. Both women start violently

Ta, love. Well? Aren't you going to tell me?
Ida I think I hear Dan coming.

Heavy footsteps are heard off

Margery I suppose I'd be better off.
Ida No, don't do that. Stay and have something to eat.
Margery Well, that's sweet of you, love, I don't mind if I do. Now that Collin's on nights, the house is awful lonely.

Ida goes to light the gas lamp (or oil lamp) with a match but after failing to strike six matches she spills the whole box over the table. Eventually, the cue is followed up by the lighting man, who brightens the stage lights very suddenly

Dan enters, soaked to the skin

The sound of the thunderstorm—strangely absent before—rises to a crescendo and almost drowns the dialogue

Dan (*shouting*) Eee, it's a right bloody night!
Ida (*shouting back*) Here, give me those wet things.
Dan It's been raining like this now for three days!

The sound of the rain stops abruptly. Ida tries to hang Dan's coat on a hook behind the door, only to find it is painted on the scenery

Hello, Marge. Hello, Grandad.
Grandad Eenin', Danall! (*He cackles venomously*)
Dan Talk about bloody cats and dogs! The water's flowing down the pit shaft like ale down yer Jed's gullet on payin' out night.
Ida Leave my relations out of it. He doesn't drink half what you put away when you're on form.
Dan I'll have a warm by t'fire.
Ida Daniel . . .
Dan Yes, love?
Ida I think there's something you ought to know.
Dan What?
Ida It's Albert . . .
Dan What about him, woman?
Ida A letter came this morning from that university place.
Dan Well?
Ida They want him to go there in September; a scholarship or something.
Dan Will 'e 'ell as like! I'll not 'ave any lad of mine gettin' fancy ideas put in 'is 'ead by a lot of overpaid layabouts.
Ida But he's set his heart on being an archaeologist.
Dan Archae—archae—what's the good of that, muckin' around in the ground for bits of bloody teapot, what kind of a life is that? He'll come down t'pit with me—and my father before him—er—like my father before his, before us—went—er . . . (*He peters out*)
Ida But he's such a sensitive lad, and think of his chest.

Dan Well, he'll bloody well have to toughen himself up then, 'cause he's coming down the pit and there's an end.

A pause. A burst of rain

Victoria enters, completely dry

Victoria (*barely audible above the din*) Who's going down the pit?

Nobody notices Victoria, and she repeats her line more loudly

Who is going down the pit?
Ida No-one, dear. Get those wet things off, tea's nearly ready.
Dan Hello, love.
Victoria (*kissing her father*) Hello, Mum. (*She kisses her mother*) Hello, Dad.
Margery Where are you working these days, Vicky?
Victoria International Stores in Gutter Street.
Margery And how's young Lionel?
Victoria Shush—Father doesn't approve.

Albert enters—also dry

Albert When will it give over. Hello, everybody! (*He gives a bad stage cough*)

The others exchange significant glances

Ida Come and warm yourself by the stove. You'll catch your death, my lad, standin' around in those wet things. (*She goes to help Albert*)

Albert takes off his coat, which is ankle-length. He removes it, partially, only to discover he has forgotten his trousers and hastily replaces the coat

Albert Thanks, Mater—I—er—hate sitting around in wet clothes—er— I—er—hope you've got plenty to eat, I'm starving.
Ida Well, we can all 'ave tea, now. Come and sit down.
Albert Let me hold the seat for you, Mother.
Margery I'll put the kettle on for more tea.

Margery goes out

Ida Come on, everybody, sit down, or it'll get cold. Come on, Grandad!

Margery enters

Margery helps Grandad to his place at the table. He cackles frequently. They take their places at the table, which has been set in the Grand Manner. Every item is inedible—plastic lettuce, plastic tomatoes, plastic ham, cardboard pork pies, china eggs, etc. The only exception is the bread and a pile of doughy buns. The teapot is obviously empty. Everybody struggles to pretend it is a splendid feast, smacking their lips over the plastic, pretending to chew it and crying "Yum, yum"

> Come on, get stuck in. Albert, eat up—put back what Nature's taken out.

Albert Yes, Mother, I can't wait.

Victoria I'm famished.

Dad pulls up his chair and in doing so knocks off a table leg, which falls with a crash to the floor. There is a sudden silence as the appalled cast realize what has happened. Dan makes an unavailing effort to replace the leg and supports the corner of the table himself

Dan I—er . . . son, I want a word with thee. What's all this about the university?

Ida Not now, Father. Let's eat our tea in peace!

Margery I see there's an extra place set.

Ida Yes, that's for Lionel, Vicky's young man. He said he might pop over after work.

Dan Who? Lionel? What sort of a bloody name is that?

Albert (*coughing ominously*) Not that fellow at the Co-op Bank? Vicky, really, can't you do better than that?

Victoria Shut up!

Dan Co-op Bank? I'll not have some toffee-nosed smart Alec from a counting house in my house, snooping and sneering.

Ida Come on, Father, he's a nice lad really--isn't he, Albert? Have a boiled egg. (*She puts one on his plate with a metallic clang*)

Albert I can't say I know him, really. He sometimes comes to pottery circle.

Ida There, that proves he's a presentable young man.

Grandfather's moustache falls into his teacup and he keeps the cup to his face while trying to restick it

Dan Who was that man who used to operate the winding gear? He was a poet. Eh, Grandad? What was his name?

Grandad Phillips. (*The sound is muffled by the cup*)

Dan Who?

Grandad Higgins.

Dan That's right. Jackson. Right pansy.

Victoria (*her mouth full of stale bun*) Ee ice oo im arver, I egg ooo.

Dan Will I 'ell as like! If that plutoprat tries any hinky pinky with our Vicky, well, I'll—I'll . . .

Victoria Ut arver! Ow—ooo—ooo is—ooo eee.

Albert Now, now, Vicky. You don't mean that.

Victoria I ooo. Oh un unnerands i eelins ahall. I an a oonan, a eal oonan! I eelins arr ike erryodyeles eeelins. Oh I ate oo awl! Oo owt et ee iv I own un ife. (*She explodes bun over everybody and bangs the table*)

The two legs at the end fall off, requiring the Cast to support the subsiding table. Terror spreads slowly

Dan Cut me—er—some more bread, Mother. And pass some more pickles, they're champion.

Ida is the mainstay of the table. She courageously frees one hand and pulls a chunk off the loaf, as there is no knife. She hands the mess to Dan

Pass up the jam, Albert . . .

There is a pause. Albert dare not free his hand, so he puts the jam pot on its side and tilts the table so that it rolls down to Dan. He ad-libs

It's still raining.

It is not, but they all latch on to this

Albert When will it stop.
Victoria Yes, it's still raining.
Ida Ay!
Margery When will it stop?

Lionel enters after a preliminary peep round the door

Lionel I hope you don't mind me butting in like this, only the door was open.
Ida Good evening, Lionel.
Lionel Good evening, Mrs Hepplethwaite, Mr Hepplethwaite, Mr Clegg-horn, Mrs Hackforth, Albert, Victoria.
Grandad Eenin', son. (*He cackles*)

Lionel slaps Grandad on the shoulder causing his wheelchair to slide under the table. He vanishes with a ghastly cry, being stopped from disappearing completely by his chin

Dan Well, sit down, now yer here.

There is no chair

Ida Put your coat by the stove to dry.
Lionel This is an interesting house. I was remarking to Miss Hepple-thwaite, I mean Victoria, only last Saturday, after we had been to the picture palace, that your terrace is one of the most idiosyncratic in the area. Wasn't I, Vicky?

Victoria does not reply as her mouth is full of bun

Ida Have a teacake. (*She cannot offer it*)
Lionel Thank you. (*He does not take it*)
Dan So, you work at the Co-op Bank, do you?
Victoria (*spitting out bun*) Yes, and he goes to Evening Institute.
Lionel Self-improvement, you know. It's the only way to get on.
Margery What do you study?
Lionel English Literature and the Metaphysical Poets.

Dan Where did poetry ever get the workin' man, eh? Do I spend all day slavin' my guts out to give you gaslight so as you can write that airey-fairy mumbo-jumbo doggerel? Ponies, shovels, and darkness—that's my bloody poetry, written in the blood and sweat of me and folks like me three miles down.

Lionel But, forgive me, Mr Hepplethwaite, that's all in the past. The young people of today are questioning this society and demanding more opportunities. Look at Albert! He's going to get to University!

He leans both hands on the table. Everyone groans

Dan We'll see about that.

Albert I'm going, Father, whether you like it or not!

Ida Albert!

Dan Mind your tongue, lad!

There is a frantic pounding on the door and shouts of "Ida, Ida, Dan, Dan, Idadan!" A voice off calls "Ssh, not yet." The noise stops

Lionel But can't you see, Mr Hepplethwaite, that the only way the working class can free itself from the intolerable burden it carries is to revolt, attack . . . (*He makes a flamboyant gesture and removes the one remaining leg of the table. For a moment he attempts to continue, but finally loses all concentration*)

The kettle whistles

Ida See to the kettle, Victoria, there's a good girl. (*A pause. She cannot leave the legless table*) Er—well—er—leave it.

The kettle is faded out. A world record pause. The sound of rain and storm fade up and then down. Rain is heard again and then silence

Albert Does anybody mind if I smoke? (*He cannot find his cigarettes*)

Ida Albert!

Dan Put that thing out this minute!

Albert I'm getting out of here. I shall be at the pub if anyone wants me. (*He does not move, frozen by the glares from the rest of the Cast*

Dan Sit down! You're not leaving here until I say so.

The sound of a hooter is heard, together with frantic pounding on the door

Jed (*off*) Ida! Ida! Dan! Dan! Ida! Dan!

Ida I'm coming, I'm coming. (*She remains seated*)

Jed Throttle and P.C. Boothroyd enter

Jed It's the pit, the pit!

P.C. Boothroyd How do, all, there's nothing to be alarmed about. There's been an accident.

Margery An accident? Where? In the pit? My Col's down there—my Colin. What's happened?

P.C. Boothroyd Calm down, Mrs Hackforth. It'll be all right, just you wait and see.

Margery He's been hurt, hasn't he? He's dead, I know it! Oh, Colin, Colin!

Margery gets up and runs out

The rest of the Cast groan under the extra weight of the table, which sags alarmingly

P.C. Boothroyd It were like this: the night shift had just gone on when they began to hear a strange rumbling sound which grew to a faint roar.

Jed (*moving to* C) I was there when it happened and it were terrible. Water burst into the pit, crushing everything. Just as I got free, the roof caved in and lots of them got drowned, poor devils. They're buried in there now—a living, watery grave. Is this what comes of a life spent slaving away at the coal face? To end, crushed by tons of rock?

Victoria There, there, Uncle Jed!

P.C. Boothroyd We need your master plan of the shafts, Mr Hepplethwaite.

Dan I'll go and get it . . . Well, er—I—uh—have it in my head.

P.C. Boothroyd Good, let's spread it out on the table.

They all pause. Ida has a flash of inspiration

Ida Maybe they need some food and drink at the pit head.

At first nobody understands her meaning, so she repeats the line and then they catch on

All Good idea! Yes, let's take the whole table! Etc., etc.

The Cast carry the table towards the door but, then, unable to get it through, walk it towards the wings and exit, leaving the P.C. and Jed

P.C. Boothroyd That's right, Mrs Hepplethwaite. You sit down by the fire, there's nought to do up there.

Jed I'll show you the best—where the—er . . . (*He stops in confusion*)

P.C. Boothroyd I'll clear the crowds for you, Mr Hepplethwaite.

A crash is heard off, as of a table being dropped

Jed Thank you, Albert. That's very kind. I could use you on the pumps.

P.C. Boothroyd Come on, then. Let's all get going. There's no time to lose!

Jed and P.C. Boothroyd exit, leaving a bewildered Grandad stranded on the stage. He cackles and makes one or two feeble moves with his wheelchair. Eventually he gives up and after staring off stage for help, suddenly leaps out of the chair and runs off

CURTAIN

ALL'S WELL THAT ENDS AS YOU LIKE IT

ALL'S WELL THAT ENDS AS YOU LIKE IT

By Michael Green
From an idea by William Shakespeare

First performed as part of The Coarse Acting Show at the Cathedral Hall, Edinburgh, on August 22nd, 1977, with the following cast:

Frederigo, a deposed Duke	David Pearson
Dronio, his son	Robin Duval
Testiculo, a clown	John Turner
Mud, a loon	Michael Langridge
Bronchio, a usurping Duke	David Crewes
Friar Crucible, a holy man	John Wilbourn
Delia, daughter to Bronchio	Margaret Turner
Lute Player	Michael Langridge
Grot, another loon	Michael Langridge
Dracula, a nurse	Ann Johnson
Messenger	Michael Langridge
The god Pan	Richard Gaunt
Bolio	Michael Langridge
Soldiers, Attendants, etc.	Richard Johnson
	Peter Macnamara
	Richard Lewis
	Sonia Pearson
	Lorna Duval

SCENE: The Forest of Solihull, the Duke's palace and elsewhere

PRODUCTION NOTES

The essence of this piece is that it must be played with total conviction, despite the fact that a lot of the lines are deliberate gibberish. After all, a hallmark of Coarse Shakespeare is that most of the cast don't understand the lines. This is especially true of a comedy where much of the humour (such as the horn jokes) has lost its point for a modern audience. Testiculo is an example. This is a difficult part because he has to be so unfunny that he becomes funny. However, there is something basically humorous in his situation, as he continues to spout rubbish which he himself plainly finds totally unfunny, but at which the cast fall about, because the director has told them to. It is most important that the cast's laughter at Testiculo's jokes and the other unfunny ones is completely excessive (another sign of Coarse Shakespeare is that there is more laughter on-stage than in the audience). At Edinburgh we played as if the piece was being done by a group none of whom wanted the dire part of Testiculo, which was therefore foisted on a downtrodden member of the society, who tried hard but who visibly winced at the worst parts and was plainly fed up. The despair with which he said the ghastly final speech usually won him a round of applause. He relieved his feelings with the bladder, with which he dealt savage blows.

Pace is important in this piece. It must not be allowed to drag.

THE FIGHT: Dronio's sword-fight with the soldiers is stock Coarse Shakespeare. A rush by the soldiers is repulsed by Dronio, who disarms them. He turns round and one tries to stab him. Dronio turns and delivers Coarse Death No. 1 (under armpit—victim crawls behind scenery gurgling). Dronio and the other soldier then do several Figure 8 parries (parry above shoulder, parry at knee level), clashing their shields together after each parry. Dronio then holds his shield over his head and a soldier hits it. Reverse roles and repeat. Lock sword hilts. Dronio drives back soldier. Soldier drives back Dronio. Soldier swings at Dronio's head. He ducks. Dronio swings at soldier's knees. He jumps. To end fight Dronio trips and falls helpless. Grunt freely. Both begin very tentatively, feebly tapping each other's swords, but then work up into a frenzy. I am grateful to Prunella Scales and Timothy West for suggesting a variation by which one fighter forgets what to do and is "prompted" by the other. Another variation might be for the Coarse Actor to play the soldier who is killed first, in addition to his five other parts. The main thing is to introduce every cliché of the stage Shakespeare fight.

ACT I

Scene 1

A part of the forest. A dense fog fills the stage

Enter Frederigo, Dronio, his son, and Testiculo, his clown

Frederigo O woe is me! Alack the day! O spite!
           Thus driven by a brother's wicked hand
           And robbed of title, palace, lands and throne
           I forced to roam the forest am at last
           Sustain'd but by my faithful followers,
           Reliant on the berries and the herbs
           For sustenance. (*He finds a berry nailed to a tree flat, and eats it with distaste*) Here will we rest awhile
           Till Phoebus marks the end of hideous day
           And then to sleep. O horror! (*He sinks down piteously*)

Dronio Be of good cheer, Father. Even though my wicked uncle, your brother the Duke of Euphoria has turned us out of our country by an evil plot and seized the throne by design yet you have a son who loves you and some followers who do likewise and the love of an honest heart is better than stewed fish on a Thursday. (*He pauses for breath*) For warmth we have the sun and for food the fruits of this Forest of Solihull; and I count them as rich as Croesus who have those. Besides we are now safe from the Duke's pursuit here in the forest and it may yet be you shall return to your palace in triumph, for Fate's wheel has many a spoke in it. Is it not so, honest clown?

Testiculo Aye marry and amen. Fart. Horn. Cuckold. (*He places his fingers on his forehead, like horns*)

Frederigo (*roaring with laughter*) Well said, brave Dronio, and as for thee, Testiculo, thou art the wittiest clown I have ever met. (*He pats him*)

Testiculo Fart. Horn. (*He strikes him with a bladder*)

Frederigo No more, I prithee, lest I die from merriment at the subtlety of thy jests. But who comes hither?

Enter the Coarse Actor in the first of his many roles, that of Mud. His costume is anything the wardrobe had left over. The crutch of his tights is round his knees. He walks with a strange gait to show he is funny

Dronio I pray thee, good man, tell us thy name.

Mud My name is Mud.

Dronio Then it were a worthy name, for thou look'st a *muddy* fellow.

They all fall about

Testiculo Fart. Horn. (*He strikes Mud with his bladder*)

There is more falling about

Dronio He is plainly a muddy man, and as mud is of the same humour
as soil, so he is near the earth and being so is out of all humours!

Further hysterical mirth

Frederigo He is as out of humours as he is out of his hose.

Testiculo He could be no sadder if he wore a pair of horns made of mud.

Frederigo Thou art too earthy.

Testiculo Earthy, say'st thou? Like a worm? An were I a worm I might
wriggle a jest with thee.

Dronio What do they call this place, O Mud?

Mud (*who has been standing patiently staring into space during all the merriment*) Soil.

Testiculo I told you he would give a muddy answer.

Mud It is called soil because there is much soil here.

    Mud exits, hobbling, mowing and gibbering

Frederigo This merriment has cheered my flagging heart,
               But for a moment only. Now night comes
               And with it thoughts as dark as molten pitch
               That make me curse the day that I was born.
               I'll take my bed.
               They sleep the best who can resign to fate
               Earth is no harder than a brother's hate.

    Frederigo exits groaning, supported by Testiculo

Dronio Resign to Fate! 'Tis easy so to say
             My father's not in love this many-a-day.
             I love my cousin Delia. Cursed be
             My wicked uncle, for it is by he
             We are both sundered now. O Delia sweet,
             I love thee. Would that we could meet.

    *Dronio turns to go with a flamboyant gesture and knocks over a card-
board tree. He exits*

Scene 2

*A part of the palace. The scene change is completed in a dim-out with a
certain amount of confusion. When the lights go up an endless fanfare
sounds and the Duke Bronchio enters with attendants, soldiers, the Friar
and Delia in an interminable procession which snakes around the stage.*

The Duke is preferably hunch-backed and limps. He carries a hunting hawk on one wrist, which he caresses from time to time. He seats himself on his throne

Bronchio Come play, musicians, ho! Some sweet song to . . .

Bronchio stops as he realizes he is partially masked by a large tree left over from the previous scene.

> *As Bronchio stops, the tree glides off as the stage-hand trapped behind it decides on flight*

(*Apprehensively*) Come play, musicians, ho! Some sweet song there to soothe—(*he pauses in case there is another interruption*)—our melancholy.

Bronchio's voice, incidentally, is Stock Shakespeare. That is, he pronounces every single syllable with great relish—saying "banishéd" for "banished" for instance, and pronouncing "-tion" as "seeon", plus any other eccentricities he can think of. He now waves towards an obvious gap in the Attendants where a Musician (or "Music-eeon" as he probably pronounces it) should be. But no music comes forth

(*With emphasis*) Come play, Musicians, ho!

No Musicians arrive, but the Sound Operator picks up the cue and appropriate music begins

> *After two or three bars the Coarse Actor bounds on stage carrying a lute. He has changed from Mud into courtier's costume, but has not had time to change his obscene tights, which are still obviously Mud's. With frenzied activity he starts plucking the strings of his lute, but they are only made of string and his hand becomes enmeshed in them. He desperately shakes his hand to free it. The music continues*

Enough, no more.

The Coarse Actor stops playing but the music goes on, so he starts up again

No more! Enough. Enow. Sufficient. Cease. Stop.

He makes "end it" motions with his hands towards the sound operator's box. The music stops abruptly in the middle of a bar. Bronchio rises to address his daughter and moves towards her as he does so

How now, daughter . . .

He stops with a strangled cry as he is brought up short by the fact that his robe is caught on a nail projecting from the throne and staggers backwards. After a brief struggle he unhooks himself

How now, daughter, methinks thou art somewhat melancholy?

Delia Indeed not, my lord.

Bronchio Indeed, I thinkst thou be so. I trust thou art not thinking of thy absent cousin Dronio again. For be it known throughout my dukedom that anyone who shall so much as speak to my banishéd brother Frederigo or his son, shall be punishéd by death!

Bronchio's voice rises to a shriek and he strikes a fierce pose which is rather spoiled by the noise of the Coarse Actor who has got his hand trapped inside his lute and is desperately trying to free it

Aware all eyes are on him, the Coarse Actor slinks off, still trying to release his hand

Friar Crucible My lord, this course of malice is untoward. Wind up your bloody flag and let fair peace reign twixt you and your brother and let this maiden here be reunited with her love, your brother's son, Dronio.

Bronchio Thou hast pronouncéd thy doom, vile cleric. (*He hurls him to the ground*) Only thy white hairs and thy robe save thee from hideous death. But banishéd thou shalt be from our domain till death do light upon thy crackéd visage. Let it be so.

    Let it be known thoughout this ducal house

    That death awaits he who would my brother's cause espouse.

The Duke showers spit in all directions and waves his arm so vigorously the hawk drops off. He does not notice but exits alone. A pause. He tip-toes back in, replaces the hawk, and exits again in character, followed by all except Delia and the Friar

Delia Oh, Father Crucible, you have sacrificed yourself for me.

In her excitement she hurls herself round his knees which have already suffered in his encounter with the Duke. The Friar cries out in pain and recovers

Friar 'Twere easy enow for one so lovely. But come, fair Delia, and trust me. I have a device to make all well twixt you and Dronio.

The Friar is savagely interrupted by the Coarse Actor blundering on stage and knocking into him. This is because he has changed into a cloak and huge cowl, the latter coming so far down over his eyes as to blind him. After the collision he pushes back the cowl to reveal the familiar features of Mud, alias Lute-player, plus a long white beard on elastic

Ah, here comes an elderly pardoner shall help us in my plan.

Delia I pray thee, worthy pardoner, what is thy name?

The Coarse Actor hastily resumes his pose as a stock old man (make-up no. 3). He pulls the cowl back over his face, stoops, saws the air meaninglessly and speaks in an incredible, quavering voice with the habit of repeating the last word of other people's lines

Grot My name is Grot. I am an elderly loon.

Delia 'Twere a worthy enough name, I trow, for thy features are pure grot, being invisible behind thy cowl, and so is thy habit, the which, being grotty out of all humours, is like a tailor's napkin, worn only round the edge.

She speaks this rubbish with great speed. The Friar and Delia fall about with mirth. Grot stares into space

The Nurse—Dracula—enters. Her performance is rather similar to that of Grot. She has a huge stuffed bosom

Delia Why, 'tis my old nurse, Dracula.

Nurse Sweet child! How lovely thou art! And how thou hast grown! I have not seen thee since you were a little suckling babe swinging upon my dugs. How she gave suck! Suck, suck, suck she went. Oh she was a thirsty baby! (*She demonstrates, using her upstage breast*)

Friar (*somewhat hastily*)

Good nurse, enow. But here's my privy plan.
This evening, when the curfew's iron tongue
Hath tolled its solemn message both of you
Must steal forth from the palace, both at once,
And use the wicket gate, the better there
To 'scape detection by the evil duke.
I shall be there to meet you. Also, Grot,
Whose white hairs do conceal an honest heart.

Grot Aye. (*He mows and saws a little*)

Delia Shall I not be recognized?

Friar I shall procur for thee some borrowed weeds, the garments of a boy.

Delia A boy? Am I to pass as a boy, then?

Friar Aye, if you wish to see your lover Dronio again. Once past the gate I shall straight convey thee to him.

Delia Oh happy day! I thank thee, holy man.

Friar The hour grows on apace. Each to our separate tasks. At curfew then. Come, honest Grot.

Grot (*gibbering again*) Aye.

Exeunt. Unfortunately Grot is blinded by his cowl and trips over his long robe, bringing down the rest of the party who are in front of him. In the chaos he reveals he has still got the lute stuck on his hand. He guiltily tries to hide it as he exits

ACT II

Scene 1

Part of the forest. The scene change is swifter and slightly less violent than before. Bird-song effects

Enter Testiculo

Testiculo Horn. Fart. Merry, I am so plagued by insects I am in as sad a case as the cheesemonger of Blackfriars. (*He sits on the stump of a tree and goes right through the top. With difficulty he extricates himself*) My master the Duke Frederigo has hied himself forth to brood solitary and his son Dronio being mad with love for Delia has hied himself forth likewise and I am thus left to provide food for insects, which I would gladly do if every bite were a cup of sack. How they bite! Their teeth are as sharp as the horns of a cuckold, which are both pointed and blunt, being on the one hand of no point at all and on the other too much pointed at. (*He pauses for a laugh. When it does not come he grimaces wearily and presses on*) But soft, who comes hither?

The Coarse Actor enters, this time as Mud. He has just managed the change but is panting rather hard with the rush. His hand is still stuck in his lute which is concealed behind his back

Why, 'tis neighbour Mud. Come, sir, where goest thou?
Mud (*panting*) To—seek—the—Duke—Frederigo.
Testiculo Why seekst thou him?
Mud There are some who would speak with him. Behold, they come.

Friar, Nurse and Delia in boy's clothing (which merely emphasises her exuberant femininity) enter

Friar Here will we rest awhile.

The Friar is interrupted by Mud, who dashes off rapidly to change for another part, revealing the lute on his hand

Testiculo Good morrow, all.
Friar Good morrow, my good fellow. I prithee tell me where we may find the banished Duke Frederigo?
Testiculo What wouldst thou with him?
Friar Myself and this good boy would speak with his son.

There is a pause and then Grot comes rushing on, having changed from Mud by putting his cloak over everything, and slapping on his beard. He has torn off the lute and now wears a bloodstained bandage on his hand

This good man is my pardoner, Grot.

Grot Aye.

Testiculo Is thy name Grot? Thou art a true Grot then, for thou hast but a Grot's worth of wit in thy countenance which being grotty enough in all conscience has as much grot in it as the purse of the butcher of Eastcheap which was found by the tailor of Spitalfields and that was enow to put a French fishmonger out of conscience by my troth. (*He hits him with his bladder*)

There is an explosion of mirth among everybody except Grot

Omnes Ha, ha, ha.

Grot (*hollowly*) Ha, ha.

Delia But tell me, good sir, doth the Duke's son flourish?

Testiculo Doth Dronio flourish? Now I'll tell you how—
> He flourisheth like a sapling in the snow
> Or like some goodly herb that fate has caused
> To grow upon a barren desert, waterless,
> In short, in brief, and coming to the point
> The good youth withereth.

Delia Is he sick?

Testiculo Marry, he is very sick.

Nurse Poor lamb! I yet remember how he swung upon my dugs as a child. Suck, suck, suck, he went . . .

Friar Enow, good woman. You say Dronio is sick?

Testiculo Aye, but of the heart. In short, he is sick for love of the Duke's daughter Delia.

Delia Ah!

Testiculo The youth swoons.

Delia Nay, 'tis nothing. 'Tis but the growing pains.

Friar Wilt take us to the Duke Frederigo straight?

Testiculo Marry, I will. As straight as the horns of a cuckold. Fart. (*He places his fingers on his forehead*)

Friar On then. Come, Grot.

Grot Aye.

Exeunt, Grot tottering

SCENE 2

Yet another part of the forest. The weather has changed and thunder, lightning, wind and rain abound plentifully. In addition, fog fills the stage once more and threatens to overwhelm the audience. From a scenery point of view the change is symbolized by merely exchanging the positions of two bushes, or some other ludicrous way

Frederigo and Dronio are discovered, cowering for shelter against the elements. Frederigo is moaning as usual

Frederigo The very elements are hateful to me now.
O woe the wretched day that I was born!
To languish here the victim of cruel fate
A brother's hatred and a tyrant's whim.
My kingdom shrunk to faithful followers two,
My son and good Testiculo, our clown.
Oh death come soon, or do not be too late
I fear a life of sorrow is my fate.
Oh death! Oh woe! Oh misery!

The noise of the storm stops abruptly

Testiculo, Delia, Friar, Grot and Nurse enter, coughing in the smoke and groping blindly

Testiculo My lord, I found these honest travellers in the forest seeking thee, and brought them to you straight.

Frederigo And wherefore shouldst these goodly people here
Seek me, the fount and author of all ills?
Perchance they come to gaze upon my face
As people do on those that Bedlam live
To smile and laugh at their unhappiness.

In an excess of misery he seizes the unhappy Friar and shakes him to and fro

Believe me, sirs, I am not worth to look upon,
A crawling dungheap full of evil things,
Abandoned by the gods, but at your service.
Come, state what miseries you have to tell.

Friar Good my lord, we have lately been at your brother's court.

Dronio Bring you any news of Delia, his daughter?

Delia (*aside*) I will tease him a little. He will not know me in these boyish weeds. (*She minces to him*) Speak you of Delia, sir?

Dronio Yes, boy.

Delia Do you not think I am like her, sir?

Dronio No. She is a girl. Thou art plainly a boy.

This is a rather unfortunate observation, as Delia is having trouble with her left bosom, which appears to have got loose from its restraints and which she is constantly adjusting during this conversation

Delia Indeed, I am a boy. But it were better you did not ask news of Delia, sir.

Dronio Why, good youth? Is she sick?

Delia Better that she were, sir. Oh, sir, Delia has fallen desperately in love with the Duke's butler.

Dronio The Duke's butler! Thou stick'st a dagger in my heart. (*He collapses sobbing on a tree trunk*)

Delia Oh, my heart will break. (*She finally gets her breast back where it* *belongs*) I must tell all. (*She taps Dronio on the shoulder*) Sir, are you sure you do not know me? (*In excess of enthusiasm she presses so far forward that her bust is almost thrust into his face*)

Dronio Yes, thou art a peevish boy.

With a gesture Delia removes that part of her dress which makes the least possible difference to her disguise, namely her hat

Delia Do you not know me now? (*Her hat falls out of her hand and drops behind her. She turns and bends down to pick it up*)

Dronio (*gazing at her rear*) Delia! 'Tis you!

Delia Dronio!

Frederigo Delia!

Friar My liege!

Nurse Sweet Dronio, dost thou not remember thy old nurse, who when you were a babe, did give you suck. These are the very dugs. (*She indicates them with unnecessary directness*)

Dronio (*with horror*) Could I ever forget, sweet nurse. But who is this worthy man who waits behind?

Grot My name is Grot. I am a loon.

Dronio Aye, thou lookest somewhat out of Grot, and being so, canst doubtless grot no more. But come, give thee good grot.

All laugh heartily, except Grot

Grot (*hollowly*) Ha, ha.

Fred But how camest thou hither?

Friar Thy wicked brother banished me for speaking in thy favour and told his daughter nevermore to think of Dronio. So I brought her hither, and together with mine own self, and the faithful Grot.

Grot Aye.

A trumpet sounds

Friar But what noise is that without?

There is a hiatus. They all look at Grot, who realizes he should have been off by now

Grot dashes off and the trumpets continue for some time to fill in the gap until he reappears as the all-purpose Coarse Messenger, having got rid of his cloak and thrust on a chain-mail hat to signify the change

Messenger Flee, my lord. The Duke Bronchio with a vast army is approaching.

The Messenger exits

Frederigo Oh woe, alack the day, oh woeful news, oh misery, of death, oh woe.

Dronio Woe.

Delia Oh horror!
Friar The gods protect us now.

They all look off expectantly

> *Bronchio enters from the other side, accompanied by an army of two*
> *small and weedy Soldiers*

Bronchio Stay, brother, nephew, daughter, Friar. Seize them!

The Soldiers do their best to comply

Delia Father, stay. Have mercy I pray thee!
Duke No mercy. Convey them hence to present execution!
Frederigo Brother!
Delia Father!
Friar My lord!
Dronio Uncle!
Nurse Good sir, I pray thee on these dugs of mine . . .
Bronchio Thy prayers are vain! Take them away!
Dronio While I have breath I will defend them all. Draw, thou murderous
   dogs!

All flee to safety. Dronio has some difficulty getting out his sword, but then
falls upon the two soldiers in a fight containing every known Shakespeare
fight-cliché (see Production Notes). One soldier is killed early on and carefully
dies behind a tree. The other, by a ruse, has Dronio on the ground at his
mercy when he is interrupted by a strange unearthly wailing which leaves
everyone spellbound

Bronchio What is this strange hum which fills the air?
Delia 'Tis like no music I ever heard before.
Testiculo If this be music let me be stuffed with a girt gurdy prickett and
   the horns too, birlady and God's sonties, for 'tis a very quondam,
   thrasonical catch to me, marry, fart and amen.
Duke Peace, fool.
Frederigo This music is belike a judgement on us for some sin. To hell
   we soon must go, oh misery, oh woe!
Friar Nay, listen, it is not the hound of hell. It hath a pleasant air.

The music grows louder

Dronio 'Tis louder. This speaks not of this world.

> *Thunder, etc., as the god Pan enters for no reason at all, probably in a*
> *flash of lightning and a puff of smoke. He wears a papier mâché goat's*
> *head through which he obviously has difficulty in seeing as it has got twisted.*
> *All kneel in deepest supplication*

Omnes Ah!
Pan Stay, foolish mortals! I am Pan, god of the forest. (*He has trouble*

with his head and collides with a tree and for a moment is out of control)
I charge thee be at peace with one another. My magic flute will charm
thee all into obedience. Come forth, my fairy Bolio, and play.

*The Coarse Actor enters, as Bolio, a fairy. If he is flown in, so much the
better. On top of the remnants of his other costumes he has wings. He
has a flute which he plays, or rather mimes, to recorded music which
rarely bears any relation to what he is doing*

All remain, spellbound

Pan Mortals all, I charge you this
    That when you wake you be at peace.
    No more strife and no more hate
    Brothers love and lovers mate.
    Hobbity gobbity trow and firk
    Let the ghoolies here not lurk.
    When the music finished be
    Come to life and friendly be.

The music ceases

    *Bolio exits. Pan tries to do so but is blinded by his false head and nearly
    dives off the front of the stage. After he has made several false starts
    Bolio returns and leads him off*

Bronchio What means this? Brother!
Frederigo Brother!
Bronchio I had a dream in which I was going to kill thee and my daughter
    Delia.
Frederigo 'Twas no dream.
Bronchio And Delia wishes to marry Dronio as in my dream?
Delia That was no dream, my lord.
Bronchio Alas, I have wrongéd thee all. Thy throne shall be restoréd and
    from henceforth the rest of my life shall be spent in contrition. Come,
    let us return to the palace to celebrate the nuptials of these young
    people. This holy man shall perform the sacred rites of Hymen.
Friar With all my heart. Come, sweet Delia, come, Nurse, let us return.
    Come, honest Grot, thy task is done.

Grot is nowhere to be seen

    Some magic has been here, I see,
    That these great men should reconciléd be.
    Come, let us go.

Exeunt omnes. Bolio enters

Bolio Now comes milk frozen home in pail

Creeping to school unwillingly like snail.
And sings the starry owl at night
Put out the light and then put out the light.

When Tom bears logs into the hall
Mewling and puking in his nurse's arms
Then shall we three meet again
Sans teeth, sans eyes, sans taste, sans everything.

It was a lover and his lass
Full of strange oaths and bearded like the bard
With a hey, and a ho, and a hey nonino,
Oh wherefore art thou, Romeo?

A merry note, tu-who, tu-whit
While greasy Joan doth have a fit.

Bolio bows, then exits. The Lights fade and go up on a typical Shakespeare curtain call in which the characters enter in order of importance, starting with the Soldiers and Attendants. Just as everyone is filing off, Pan blunders blindly on stage and tries to feel his way to the front. He is dragged off by Bolio

GENERAL NOTE ON THE SETTINGS

The four plays may be presented as simply or as elaborately as facilities permit.
The following items are necessary to the action:

Il Fornicazione: Window, door
Streuth: French windows, fireplace, door, "wobbly" flat
A Collier's Tuesday Tea: Door
  For furniture, etc., see appropriate plots.

IL FORNICAZIONE
FURNITURE AND PROPERTY LIST

On stage: 4 ornate chairs
Small table. *On it:* sewing materials
Large table. *On it:* ornate papier-maché goblets and jugs, plates, cutlery, cruet

Off stage: Triangle **(Musician)**
Baton **(Conductor)**
Dead stag **(Attendants)**
Trick pie with steam effect **(Countess)**
3 huge bundles of flowers **(Attendant)**
1 small bouquet **(Attendant)**

Personal: **Countess:** Vial

LIGHTING PLOT

Property fittings required: nil
Interior. A living-room

To open: General interior lighting
No Cues

EFFECTS PLOT

Cue 1	**Countess:** "But, beloved—hark!"	(Page 7)
	Hunting horn sounds	
Cue 2	**Maid:** ". . . with his hunting party."	(Page 8)
	Hunting horn sounds, louder	
Cue 3	Preceding **Count's** entrance	(Page 8)
	Loud blast on horn, followed by baying and howling dogs	
Cue 4	After **Count** is borne off	(Page 11)
	Loud crash	

STREUTH
FURNITURE AND PROPERTY LIST

On stage: Settee

Drinks table. *On it:* various drinks, assorted glasses (one already filled), telephone

Will ⎫
Poker ⎭ for Corpse

Off stage: Bundle of old clothes **(Vicar)**

Personal: **Hubert:** wristwatch, 2 cigarette cases
Inspector: notebook, ball-point pen, handkerchief

LIGHTING PLOT

Property fittings required: nil
Interior. A Drawing-room

To open:	General interior lighting	
Cue 1	**James:** "I ran in ere."	(Page 21)
	Fade to single Spot, just missing James	
Cue 2	**James:** "DEAD!"	(Page 22)
	Fade Spot and return to opening lighting	
Cue 3	**Inspector:** "Like this." He turns off switch second time	(Page 22)
	Pause, then snap Black-out	
Cue 4	**Inspector** falls over corpse	(Page 22)
	Snap Lights on full, as opening	

EFFECTS PLOT

Cue 1	Before and as CURTAIN rises	(Page 19)
	Music—"Mars" from Holst's Planets *suite*	
Cue 2	**Inspector:** ". . . how do you explain . . ."	(Page 25)
	Telephone rings	

A COLLIER'S TUESDAY TEA
FURNITURE AND PROPERTY LIST

On stage: 5 wooden chairs

Large trick table. *On it*: cloth, bread on board, trick bread-knife, cutlery and dishes for 4, jam pot, empty teapot, box of matches' plastic lettuce, tomatoes, ham, cardboard pork pies, china eggs, etc· —all inedible—plate of doughy buns. (*See Author's Note*)

Wheelchair with detachable wheel. (*See Author's Note*)

Stove

LIGHTING PLOT

Property fittings required: gas lamp, stove glow effect
Interior. A Living-room

To open:	Black-out	
Cue 1	As Curtain rises	(Page 33)
	Fade up to warm, rather dim lighting and glowing stove	
Cue 2	Music stops	(Page 33)
	Start general fade, hesitate, then bring up to opening lighting	
Cue 3	**Ida** fails to strike matches	(Page 34)
	Brighten lighting overall	

EFFECTS PLOT

Cue 1	As Curtain rises	(Page 33)
	Music—continue until Cast find correct positions	
Cue 2	As music stops	(Page 33)
	Violent thunderclap, heavy rain—then silence	
Cue 3	**Ida** gives **Margery** tea-cup	(Page 33)
	Loud crash	
Cue 4	**Dan** enters	(Page 34)
	Loud thunderclap and rain	
Cue 5	**Dan**: "... for three days!"	(Page 34)
	Rain stops suddenly	
Cue 6	**Dan**: "... and there's an end."	(Page 35)
	Pause—then tremendous burst of rain	
Cue 7	**Lionel** loses all concentration	(Page 38)
	Kettle whistles	
Cue 8	**Ida**: "—leave it."	(Page 38)
	Kettle fades out. Long pause. Rain and storm fade up and down. Rain again. Then silence	

Cue 9   **Dan: "... until I say so."**   (Page 38)
             Hooter sounds
Cue 10   **Boothroyd: "... for you, Mr Hepplethwaite."**   (Page 39)
             Loud crash
Cue 11   As Lights fade   (Page 39)
             Music

ALL'S WELL THAT ENDS AS YOU LIKE IT
FURNITURE AND PROPERTY LIST

ACT I

SCENE 1

On stage: Various trees, bushes and stumps

Off stage: Clown's bladder **(Testiculo)**
　　　　　Staff **(Coarse Actor)**

SCENE 2

Strike:　All trees except one

Set:　　Large throne

Off stage: Lute **(Coarse Actor)**

ACT II

SCENE 1

Strike:　Throne
Set:　　Various trees, bushes, stumps (1 hollow)

SCENE 2

Set:　　2 previous bushes in different positions

Off stage: Flute **(Coarse Actor)**

LIGHTING PLOT

Property fittings required: nil
Parts of a Forest: Part of a Palace

ACT I.　Day

To open:　General exterior lighting
Cue 1　　At end of Scene 1　　　　　　　　　　　　(Page 46)
　　　　　Black-out
Cue 2　　When ready　　　　　　　　　　　　　　(Page 46)
　　　　　Bring up general lighting, concentrated on throne

ACT II.   Day

to open:	As start of Act I	
Cue 3	As Scene 1 closes	(Page 51)
	Change to storm effect	
Cue 4	Storm ceases abruptly	(Page 52)
	Brighten overall lighting	
Cue 5	**Pan** enters	(Page 54)
	Flash of lightning	
Cue 6	**Bolio** bows	(Page 56)
	Fade to Black-out, then up to full for CURTAIN CALL	

EFFECTS PLOT

Cue 1	On **Dronio's** exit	(Page 46)
	Music to cover scene change	
Cue 2	**Bronchio:** ". . . play musicians, ho!" (3rd time)	(Page 47)
	Lute music	
Cue 3	**Coarse Actor** signs to Sound Operator	(Page 47)
	Stop lute music abruptly	
Cue 4	At start of Act II, Scene 1	(Page 50)
	Bird-song effect	
Cue 5	At start of Act II, Scene 2	(Page 51)
	Thunder, lightning, rain, wind	
Cue 6	**Fred:** "Oh misery!"	(Page 52)
	Storm stops abruptly ·	
Cue 7	**Grot:** "Aye."	(Page 53)
	Trumpet sounds	
Cue 8	**Soldier:** Has Dronio on ground	(Page 54)
	Strange unearthly wailing	
Cue 9	**Dronio:** ". . . not of this world."	(Page 54)
	Thunder—puff of smoke	
Cue 10	As **Bolio** plays flute	(Page 55)
	Music—ad lib	
Cue 11	**Pan:** ". . . and friendly be."	(Page 55)
	Music stops